Concrete Mixers

BY JEAN EICK

The Child's World®

Published by The Child's World®
1980 Lookout Drive • Mankato, MN 56003-1705
800-599-READ • www.childsworld.com

Acknowledgments
The Child's World®: Mary Berendes, Publishing Director
The Design Lab: Design
Jody Jensen Shaffer: Editing
Pamela J. Mitsakos: Photo Research

Photos
BanksPhotos/iStock.com: 15; BMXForever/iStock.com:
11; Design-Smart.com/iStock.com: 20; Henk Jacobs/
Shutterstock.com: 12; kozmoat98/iStock.com: 16;
OMcom/Shutterstock.com: 7; Qingwa LLC/iStock.
com: 8; Richard Thornton/Shutterstock.com: 4; Robert
Pernell/Shutterstock.com: 19; XPhantom/Shutterstock:
cover, 1

ISBN 9781623239640
LCCN 2013947250

Printed in the United States of America
Mankato, MN
November, 2013
PA02190

Contents

This concrete mixer
is being used
to build a bridge.

What are concrete mixers?

Concrete mixer trucks stir and carry **concrete**. Concrete is almost like stone. It is used for building many things. It is used in making sidewalks, basements, walls, and roads.

How is concrete made?

Concrete is made by mixing water, **cement**, sand, and small stones. The wet cement acts like paste. It holds the sand and stones together. As the mixture sits, it gets hard. It also gets very strong.

Concrete is wet
and gloppy
before it hardens.

7

cab

steering wheel

engine

299

299

What are the parts of a concrete mixer?

Some parts of concrete mixer trucks look like other trucks. The driver sits in a **cab**. The truck has an **engine**. The engine makes power that moves the truck. The driver uses the steering wheel to turn the truck.

The back looks much different from other trucks! A big **drum** holds the concrete. The drum turns around and around. As the drum turns, big **blades** inside stir the concrete.

drum

This worker is spraying water on the chute.

How are concrete mixers used?

A concrete mixer truck takes concrete where workers need it. The truck slowly backs up. Workers pull out the truck's **chute**. They place it where they want the concrete to go.

To mix the concrete, the drum turned one way. Now it is time to pour the concrete. The drum spins the other way. The blades push the concrete out instead of mixing it.

The gooey concrete can pour out quickly!

Concrete becomes harder to spread around as it dries.

The concrete pours down the chute. Workers use tools to push the concrete into place. They work quickly. They must hurry before the concrete gets hard.

At last, all the concrete is out of the truck. The workers put the chute back into place. The concrete mixer leaves. It is ready for its next job.

This concrete mixer
is moving on
to its next job.

19

This concrete mixer is being used on a construction site.

Are concrete mixers useful?

Concrete is used all over the world. It is used in all kinds of building. Concrete mixers are a big help for mixing and carrying concrete. They are very useful!

GLOSSARY

blades (BLAYDZ) Blades are things that are broad, flat, and often thin.

cab (KAB) A machine's cab is the area where the driver sits.

cement (suh-MENT) Cement is a fine dust made from ground-up rocks.

chute (SHOOT) A chute is a slide.

concrete (KON-kreet) Concrete is a mixture of water, cement, sand, and small stone.

drum (DRUM) A drum is a bin for holding something.

engine (EN-jun) An engine is a machine that makes something move.

BOOKS

Brill, Marlene. *Concrete Mixers.* Minneapolis, MN: Lerner Publications, 2007.

Dussling, Jennifer. *Construction Trucks.* New York: Grosset & Dunlap, 1998.

Froeb, Lori. *Super Concrete Mixer.* Pleasantville, NY: Reader's Digest Children's Books, 2005.

McClellan, Ray. *Concrete Mixers.* Minneapolis, MN: Bellwether Media, 2007.

WEB SITES

Visit our Web site for lots of links about concrete mixers:
childsworld.com/links

Note to parents, teachers, and librarians: We routinely check our Web links to make sure they're safe, active sites—so encourage your readers to check them out!

INDEX

ABOUT THE AUTHOR

Jean Eick has written hundreds of books for children. She has written biographies, craft books, and many titles on nature and science. Jean enjoys hiking in the mountains, reading, and doing volunteer work.